THE STUNTMAN

THE STUNTMAN

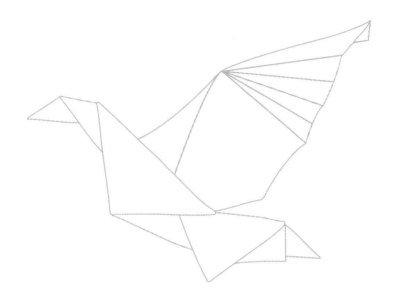

POEMS

BRIAN LAIDLAW

MILKWEED EDITIONS

Published 2014 by Milkweed Editions
Printed in the United States of America
Cover design by Mary Austin Speaker
Author photo by Colin Kopp
15 16 17 18 19   5 4 3 2 1
First Edition

Milkweed Editions, an independent nonprofit publisher, gratefully acknowledges sustaining support from the Jerome Foundation; the Lindquist & Vennum Foundation; the McKnight Foundation; the National Endowment for the Arts; the Target Foundation; and other generous contributions from foundations, corporations, and individuals. Also, this activity is made possible by the voters of Minnesota through a Minnesota State Arts Board Operating Support grant, thanks to a legislative appropriation from the arts and cultural heritage fund, and a grant from the Wells Fargo Foundation Minnesota. For a full listing of Milkweed Editions supporters, please visit www.milkweed.org.

Library of Congress Cataloging-in-Publication Data

Laidlaw, Brian, 1983-
  [Poems. Selections]
  The stuntman : poems / Brian Laidlaw.
     pages cm
  ISBN 978-1-57131-464-2 (paperback) -- ISBN 978-1-57131-910-4 (ebook)
  I. Title.
  PS3612.A397A6 2015
811'.6--dc23
                                                    2014033907
                                                                          CIP

Milkweed Editions is committed to ecological stewardship. We strive to align our book production practices with this principle, and to reduce the impact of our operations in the environment. We are a member of the Green Press Initiative, a nonprofit coalition of publishers, manufacturers, and authors working to protect the world's endangered forests and conserve natural resources. *The Stuntman* was printed on acid-free 30% postconsumer-waste paper by Versa Press.

To A.B.C. Finch

THE STUNTMAN

II.

I was born at the bottom of a wishing well.

BOB DYLAN
"Motorpsycho Nightmare"

THE STUNTMAN

[Telegram]

THE EARTH BROKE OPEN CAUSE WE BROKE IT OPEN, FIRE CAME OUT IN THE
FORM OF AIR

EARTH IN THE FORM OF FIRE WAS OPENING MOUTHS,
A BYSTANDER TURNED INTO A TREE, WITH SHOCK I SHOOK IT

I WANTED TO STUPEFY EARTH WITH MY FINESSE, LAY IT OUT ON MY
BLANKET & FEED IT GRAPES

I.

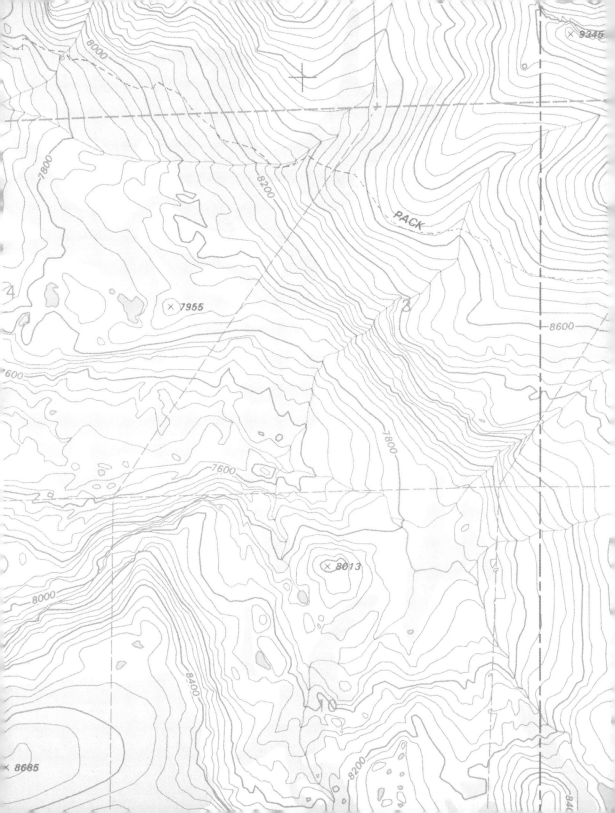

[*Narcissus the Debutante*]

newcomer grows in, killing familiarity
the wealthy scramble to incorporate

he attends their dinners
like demons they need new bodies

downlooker comes to town, comes to their parties
they think him shy

no, he knows there's no such thing as eye contact

the wolf has a horizontal sweet spot on its retina
for spotting prey on the prairie

the stranger has a narcissus
shaped sweet spot

all the better to spot himself

here is his typewriter retina,
he swaggers from ocular to oracular

to alienate everyone comprehensively, encyclopedically
is to become, in essence, alien

[*Dotted Lines*]

he bursts the windows round him
he dreams

                    of being tenfold or a hundredfold

like a paper airplane bent
into a paper bird

//

                              (*over the mainline highway,*
                                  the low-lain bypass)

he beaks his neck to his chin
he folds his neck up and down

                    but I don't care,
            that man's never becoming a swan

[Voyeurs Cum Voyageurs]

you know the first fucks

here were trappers
they dealt in pelts,

they sold chambers

of meatless animal
& mortal coil

here coal stains, here gun grease
mingles with bear grease

but so what

if you sleep in a hundred deaths:
beech, birch, beaver dam, bear-dam

we lowdown our hearts in the tundra
we lowdown the spades

& just when we think no one is watching

everybody is

[*A List of Scenarios*]

a bird with a broken wing

"two bars walk into a downtown"

the piano is under lock & key

nobody on the riverbank knows what "riparian" means

grand canyon as eyesore

a bird that is only a wing

hollywood (i assume) was once wooded with holly

people identify themselves with dances rather than names

the obelisk song

"i remember the pre-nostalgia era"

you discover you are "that guy"

the randomizer stalks the spreadsheet

the new york times review of intentions

letters to a young undertaker

[Echo's Dogs]

You grew up with 30-plus
Different dogs with names like "Little Dog" and "Latecomer."

(The time between being a puppy and being
a dead dog is called "life.")

You will recall
When you wanted to know what *missing* feels like,
I said "hunger,"

And you said "for a person?"
And then you said "like cannibalism?"

And then I said "yes."

[*Domestic Spacerace*]

I like it when I look out a window

and can't see any other windows. Ours is a simple joy,

clinking glasses.

So what if they demoted Pluto;

it's still on the rocks, and it's also still

neat to me.

Dear life, thanks

for being my life.

Hubble glints out there like a pond, a proud American eye.

Clinking glasses is how focus works,

like a matter of fact

of distance, like I like it when I look out a window

and see you in the yard.

[Home of the Standstill Parade]

It was a hard freeze we were up north there were fishhouses
decorated to look like only fish or only houses there were kids
grappling with a lot of candy my sister was there
nobody cared about the wattage of anything the streetlamps were dull
as knives in candle light it's not just that your uncle
was drunk it was everyone had a drunk uncle the fish float
was built on a hay wagon dragging down the main
drag throwing candy wet inside the wrapper your discomfort is contagious
unearthly sounds propelled the motorcade I am
wondering if it's deadly to eat dry ice I might be eating it now my tongue is numb
like it's someone else's I think tonguing oneself
is a simulacrum of death by overexposure the fishhouse floats
keep coming they have hooks in their mouths made from coat-
hangers Jesus easily feeding the millions with a croppy
the size of a humpback hands freezing
into clubs cardboard fins freezing into usable blades breakfast
will be blubber and apologies
breakfast will be painkillers and mingy water awe Jesus awe Jesus the frostbit lure
is making an appearance in your mother's mouth
contagion is a currency isn't it, pain
relief is a currency the fish is wearing a fisherman hat he
is driving wasted the streetlights are cutting him
how is this town exclusively
mothers and uncles who makes what besides Miller and Marlboro here is a float
the shape of a sunken ship here are ten adults dressed as children
here is vice, here versa
here are the lights going out in front of one man walking
here is a man a little later thinking the whole world is
dark, whose blood is in my mouth here I am flattered
here I heard there was a river but I heard no river
here are the fishhouses leaving here is a frozen parade of houses
called a home on the range here are countless stationary
humans with a town moving through them their lips are chattering like windows

[*Tract House Jingle*]

The good part about parallel roads
is they never

make a crossroads.
Roads like Adam & Eve

not talking or touching,
back to back,

roads with their cocks out
but unperturbed.

I know who
invented the grid system, who

decided on *perpendicular*—
the devil is a salesman

needing a block to sell around.
He has a steel

just-for-you guitar
with six strings attached.

You used
to be a babe, babe,

& I wrote a song that goes
almost like this.

[Upstate Mothers' Refrain]

I know all the dishware is stain glass, all the laundry's rosy wash
I know our well & our iron are all we have
I know one sameness

let's imagine iron turns everything red, no, i don't have to imagine

I know our red teeth are dull red
I know where the rabbit pauses to overlook & decide it's not worth it, goodbye

mother chops wood, so does brother

I know her trapezoid makeup, her charming footing
I know we come across as sickly in our fortifications
I know the pump & contemplate *flush*, contemplate *roan*

mother chops wood, so does brother

I know the tart iron water is reaming the well-poles
I know freshwater sharks
I know haters & orphans
I know patriot atheists

let's imagine iron turns everything red, no, i don't have to imagine

I know the toilet bowl is rubylike
I know we are good neighbors
I know we are low on the list of places to bomb
I know our bloody hair

mother chops wood, so does brother

I know fruitless toil &

I know god like a foreman
I know pride like an animal circling a carcass &
I know no anemics

let's imagine iron turns everything red, no, i don't have to imagine

I know mothers staring out windows counting days till something auspicious befalls them
I know it is pointless to clean when our blood looks so clean & our water looks so dirty
I know mothers who, like fire, work till the instant they die

[Spurring]

I have been staring at the sun long enough I'm ready to be the sun, the red-tailed hawk subsumed in it, it's so good the way bird-meat drips off a bird-bone in sufficient heat but it's grisly to think the same on a person

I wish I could plant feathers & grow wings in the ground, actually sometimes it works that way, actually sometimes I can

Horses are running through fields of sprung wingspans but they aren't like Pegasus, they are more like cars, exhaust comes out of their nostrils, plugs of tobacco are in their wakes, they fancy themselves breaking through French doors every time they step up, whatever gallop or enterprise

I knee through glassblowers' brick kilns where glass horseshoes are farried, riding out of the firepit & into the fire, riding out of the sunset & into the sun

[Terrarium Letter #1]

You could be a train wreck and still be marriageable, the blue jays around you are mirthy bridesmaids, their combs heft beauty into your locks, the barren fjord has a broke-ass moon splayed helplessly in it. You never were fancy or stable, like a plain rocker. Your mane is a long unwoven rope walking itself around on a short unwoven rope.

You say you live in a cabin on a raw acre on an island in Greenwich Village, well, I'll be proud to be privy, to be part of your very lunar, laminar downfall. I'll probably take your hand during it & release it soon after & regret it soon after after—

Hemming is hawing, hemming is darning, darning is damning, we could chat shit until day reassembles day, like a broke-ass fjord of light, like a puzzle of which the assembler is also a piece.

[The Cartographer Cries into His Knapsack]

My song takes the form of papier-mâché made out of maps molded into the hills the maps depict; the maps are not making me cry per se, I am making me cry thinking about the maps

        I want to hear my elegy for everywhere, over the radio in the off-road limousine, wrenching up to a place I have no business, a sing-along

        to myself weeping with joy

I will take the implausible to the bank or the courthouse & marry it there, I know you're all around me, how does a man made of reflective glass ever look in a mirror,

        the lakes glance

        off my shoulders, I mold a mashup of my cabin out of newsprint photos of other cabins, I have a proposal

if we drop into the center of everything & decide that point is just outside our screen door, then every threshold we cross thereafter crosses into our home.

II.

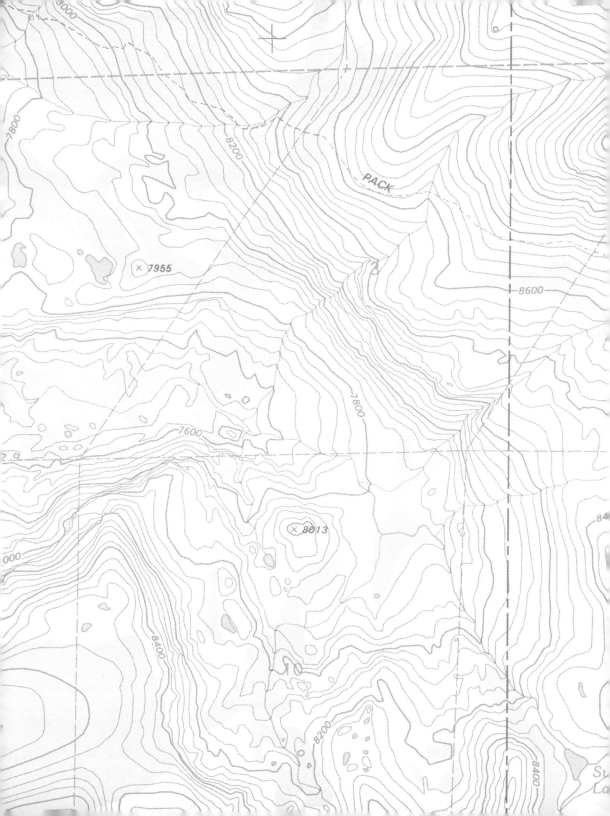

[*Narcissus the Stuntman*]

there he is with his stepchildren there he is on the moon there he is in shades that make him look like an asshole,

there he is eating hormonal meat there in traffic there his heart's gone everywhere his head has

you blew your lode in calling the twenties "modernity"

dragging his red muscle around like a goldfish in a plastic sac looking for something sharp to say it with

if not modernity then where do I live, I don't hate it I just distrust it, in my line of work I need metadata like I need a haircut meaning not at all,

reckoning without method is *dead reckoning*, my hands get stuck between stones

echo is undoing echo, echo is unbecoming echo

when the city was torn down the valley was an echoless place, I went there today, everything made by grandfathers looked shoddy but all-encompassing.

[Terrarium Letter #2]

Well the record came on & it sounded like there was a girl whistling through wooden toy horses, clack, clack, I'm no daddy but I was willing to pantomime (there's no girl either remember we're acting) the butcher leitmotif comes on, from a checklist nobody chooses ART-LIFE over LOVE-LIFE knowingly, everytime your eyes close

houses topple under the lidlets, the Trojan horse muscular & full of a stealthy shitstorm, I'm acting out all capitals, from out the owl hole a fist emerges punching your face & then opens up to reveal a tiny owl,

that's what happens when you think on purpose, LOVE-LIFE and ART-LIFE awake for hundreds of hours, the father (imaginary, played by a woman) crashes onstage, breaks the toy-horse ocarinas, *I thought lilac petals were bigger than this,*

how can so many voices not fail to double-negate each other less than they already aren't, that's what ART-LIFE and LOVE-LIFE do in private

the record needle has dust, is an eyelet, a stinger, isn't stingy, the coronets on the record are dumber than ever, the daughter falls in love with her own hands because they can't desert her or grow up or turn out to be imaginary, the farmer falls in love with the toy horses, that's how we made the record go.

Hope you're done folding that laundry, we need costumes that look like the Cold War is over, & thanks for asking.

[*If I Had a Rock*]

the community comes to community sings, sings
if I had a rock I'd rock it in the morning

no separation of churchyard & schoolyard
their ranks were crude downtown

Trotskyites were about to exist
honeys' wedding dresses upheld by chickenwire

commercial space
travel's about to exist, they capitalize on the moon though it lies
on the limns

brutality is a value for men but not families

you do whatever "cocks your revolver"

such as "cock your revolver"

soon there's no community
sing (echo is an eventuality in dead

space), soon I will love you

like I love this town, meaning
if I had a rocket I'd rocket in the morning

[*Altitude Sickness*]

Somedays I believe the idiots & impingers of me
are gradually getting smarter, the pinecone slowly unfolds,

is edible to squirrels but not humans: the pinecone flowers
like a rose & is beautiful,

but not the way a rose is. Statuesque, picturesque,
I will myself

to pan in, to want close-ups, to understand a path the way the ant does,
on kneepads & underneath objects

ten times my weight. Today

I don't wish I were in outerspace, where a torn glove means evacuation
into a void,

tonguing the peaceful regulator: today the dummies ripple around me,
I am part of the collective

idiocy, the anthill a commons & a summons.
I don't know what everybody does all day, what suits & amalgams,

but neither does anybody.

[*Crop Circles*]

only by leaving the planet

did we suspect we had been on one

only by leaving a realm did the realm re-ravel

into something nontrivial

the cloud shadows

cleave to one big shadow

whatever sex happens happens under it

whoever wages wars

wages under it

the warplanes' formations hold hands

they are unlike love

they are like information

[Telegram]

I WOULD BE WILLING TO LIVE IN A RED RADIO FLYER, MAKE BRISTLY WINGS
LIKE A DRAGON- OR BUTTERFLY OUT OF STRAW, MAKE A THATCH HOUSE TO
KISS YOU IN

A LOCKUP COMES ANYTIME YOU THINK ABOUT A DOOR, THAT'S HOW IT IS
IN IMAGINATIONLAND

IF YOU'RE BLEEDING YOU'RE BLEEDING, THAT'S HOW CAUSALITY WORKS IN
AN ENVIRONMENT

THE UNREPENTANT RED FLYER IS A MOUTHFUL OF BLOOD, WAR MUST BE
FUNNY BECAUSE PEOPLE STILL CAN LAUGH

ISN'T THAT HOW WORKING WORKS, A STICK CAN BE A STEERING WHEEL OR
A GUN, IT CAN BE SELFLESS, SOMETIMES I PRETEND IT'S YOUR HAND

[Forest Fire Song]

it's almost cannibalistic
to make a paper tree

the green paper
amounts to itself

the cavalry rise, the bugle
is a musical bludgeon

the hazardous pulp
was letting your blood

stay where it was
that's the danger

it's almost cannibalistic
to play the saws musically

a throat is
a warbling

part the saw mimics
& then approaches

the juniper, fractal,
huddling, witness

to the universe
from its center

saturn has rings,
conifer has rings

but I'm ringless
nor gravity nor age

adorn me
what is my moniker,

where was I when that
misnomer struck

the scaly juniper cajoling
(it's almost cannibalistic)

the scarry juniper cavorting
(it's almost) the careless

juniper contorting
(cannibalistic)

I am taps, I am not flashy
the cannibal song

feeds on song, the town
tastes delicious

to the town
you show up at daybreak

to roughen my door-
step

I would like to dance you
like a candelabra

I would like the pit
to catch fire like a ring

of fire & I would like to
hold your hand next

to it (cannibalistic)
prepositions bring

your hand beside it
(almost) the forest

becomes a candelabra
& I want to hold

your hand right in it

[*Altitude Wellness*]

The heavens are there whether you're in a building,
outdoors, covered in bugs, in a plum orchard, nevertheless

sometimes the jumpsuit or spacesuit of concerns
upon you sloughs off.

The serene make awful drivers.
I saw a road get driven right through a mountain however

a roadside tarpark is no place for a heavens to hide.
I pretend I have no muscles or bones falling from a height,

that no concerns like truckers or the mercantile
leap into my body from the highroad:

when we hit the ground it's like a snowfall, love, like a windfall

[Terrarium Letter #3]

I should keep a record of poetry's death in my dumb-dumb heart, I don't see humans cry at poetry readings nor humans attend them. The Twins are ok this year, corn subsidies are cheapening the bourbon, Mr. Pocket was the last person I saw cry and he was pretending to be his grandmother at the time, waving goodbye through a truck window. (The truck had cancer.)

"Where am I going with this," he said. Also, "Failure to try is the biggest failure."

Tell me what the billboards say in Wyoming, I've driven thru but I couldn't read back then.

[Male Anatomy]

I make a reasonable home for all my guts
in my body

carry them   (*not malignantly*)
I guess gallantly
up in this backwards river   (*like irrigation*)
                                    (*where should I long for*)
                                    (*if not for home*)
yes & but
where should I go
to long for it   (*Napoleon stomach*)
                                    (*Khan loin*)

sometimes I fear I have an Abraham heart,
a Kennedy fracture

                          (*too congressional*)
                          (*spilling light*)
                          (*into the arboretum*)

                          (*behind the ear*)

[Mill Fire Song]

it's the thin, magicless wall I chisel away at
between myself & all that magic

>> (*I bet heaven is over there*)
>> (*I hear footsteps*)

>> (*tinkering thru glass shards*)

the man uses sandpaper to sand his limbs

the sandpaper's made of diamond, also the limbs

>> (*internal conflict escalates itself*)

>> (*along its lines, flour is a combustible,*)

the X is a marker of thinness

between realms, (*the beams hewn roughly, the initials*)
>> (*riddling their way out*)

the scallop wall & shutters, the shuddering wall, the decidedly
concave mill-shape of the wall,

>> (*then*)

>> (*god & his polyphony are smooth*)
>> (*up to the point of absence,*)

then

(the scallop wall & shutters, the shuddering wall, the decidedly)
(concave mill-shape of the wall,)

then

the balletic flamed-out absence
of any sort of wall

[Terrarium Letter #4]

I don't like stasis, I never go to the shop that sells it, the birds are filterless in song, the cigarettes are filterless in their assault on my misery & health

Whose cig-litter litters my porch, whose lead paint

The only beach is performed by shattered windows
(I guess I'll build my glass castle)

The birds have stones from their stonefruits, imperfect pitches, they ramble, flown through my retentive frame, an inside-out silence

Crazes come & go, please, I am a reverse mime, everyone outside this imaginary glass box's not-glass is not talking

[Courtesy Call]

hey look the poems don't accomplish anything

you peel away layer after layer of skin, thinking

that's what you're made of, anatomy textbook

unfurling, bony whittled core,   emergent, your

surprise seems almost hilarious, auto-dissection

actually hurts the self,   a poem is a telephone

with a dead battery, at the bottom of the ocean

no reception (what's the sound of one call not

ringing),   your suffering is the only part about

you that I don't love   & I'm calling you on it

[Telegram]

VANDALS ARE FAILED POETS; POETS ARE FAILED VANDALS

I AM WATCHING THE TOWN CHEW ITS OWN FOOT OFF

MALICE HAS NOTHING TO DO WITH IT; MALICE ITSELF IS NOTHING

SOME DAYS I WOULD ACQUIESCE TO THE AMPUTATION OF MY GUITAR
HAND, JUST FOR THE JOY OF GETTING IT SEWN BACK ON

MY SPIRIT ANIMAL IS EVERY ANIMAL

AMERICA DENOUNCES ANYBODY DISCONTENT WITH BEING A NOBODY

DEAR FRIEND, HELP YOURSELF, PICK YOURSELF UP, PICK THE WINDSHIELD
OUT OF YOUR ARM

III.

[Narcissus the Anarchist]

Some things you love forever: destruction, yourself,

America, genitals

they are the chandeliers of your everlasting hallway,

they never transition from

match to matchless, from gas to electric. Yes at first

you were a novelty,

but who isn't; it gets so luminous you forget

how a candle smells,

forget how much it moves like a monarch butterfly

with a foot stuck in a pond of hardening or soften-

ing blood. You move, in turn, more like an anarch-

ist in the indoor

eaves, building buildings out of fire, & building fire.

[*Brain Drain*]

i

I wanted to kill the town. I did so

by not caring
the lights go out, you hear hunting dogs wagging their fingers

& the light switch
wasn't invented

so everyone's pulling cords & stepping into the miry street.

To quote Echo:
You are all mine

iron mountain,

You are all mine.

ii

I have you in my clutches,
a reflection

is a visual Echo,

a refrain is an aural reflection, & yet

you can't upstage
the man cutting his face off

in the proscenium—
some acts

are performed only once,
but certain acts

can be performed only once.

iii

Like deforestation porn,
or the *bunny* as *bunny*

becoming *rabbit* as *meat*
nobody shits

bricks over "peak iron"

do they?

The seabed fails to contain the sea;
Echo is a confrontation,

a sound holding hands with a solid, & holding perhaps
a brick in that hand.

iv

She gauges the range & the arc
up to my tenement window,

we're not kicking habits,

we're kicking each other.
(The world is all mine.)

v

A PUPPET IS PARTWAY BETWEEN
A CHARACTER AND A PROP

(That's the blurb on the back
of the human condition.)

vi.

Iron's too heavy to fly, copper may be essential
to the circuitry that enslaves us

but even the dumb *loon* as *loon*
(the *loon* as dumb *avatar*)

has got the sense to elope,
shitting white shit &

knowing which way south is.

[*Bad Language*]

I have bled with the best of them & like them
I flatter myself

bodiless, I don't remember my baptism
I was twentyone at the time you see

I hate writings that *take place*.
The sleeves of a vest must be cutoff or else it isn't a vest.

Why do I & everyone prefer eagles to geese,
wolves to dogs,

ignoble migrations, turdlike shits?
I saw an eagle kill a pigeon midflight

I never saw a goose do that.
One must pack bags in order to have packed bags.

Come help me sort out *causality* from *casualty*,
I allow myself one daypack, one backpack, one instrument.

What the geese do isn't singing,
what the eagles do isn't "merely."

The eagle regurgitates to feed its young,
the dog regurgitates its tall grass in the grass.

Come tell me what I forgot in the larder while I'm packing.
I prefer cults to religions.

I prefer bad language to language.

[Terrarium Letter #5]

So-and-So is the next So-and-So, I wonder if that's enough or if I care at all, *Is that a feather, is that a mirror, is that my car, is a commuter culture a culture?*

: : : and other questions : : :

The phrase "the gray-haired man" refers to everyone now. The cocktail tables wilting under the war recollections.

We met in Paris, everyone slept with my idol except for me, I was writing letters to friends in Breckenridge where I have no friends.

But hope springs eternal, old dogs eat old tricks for supper, you know all of this. Good luck finding your wallet.

[Notes for a Song Called "All It Takes"]

All it takes is a radio broken open & the orchestra in there playing a tattoo,
turning into taps:
the day doesn't just break, it outright shatters.
Little cymbals,
you're kissing all the right friends & they love it & none of the wrong ones.

The sunshine resembles a splay of legs in stereo.
All it takes is all your friends, (a village), a thousand compliments.
Fire shoots out of your feet like your body is a rocket—
No thanks honey I'm my own stabilizer now.

All it takes is a hundred bottles
tuned to major intervals playing waltzes; the television licks
its own adapter & dies, the dark
pointless cloud begins to make a point.

[*If We Dig Up the Overworld*]

⁓

you say you foresaw misery, well
that is safe

        (we were born with knuckles for a reason)

        (no nerves are in them for a reason)

like the bulls were pierced for a reason & like for a reason
the ground is red

⁓

if we dig up the overworld there
won't be an underworld

then death stops   (death always *stops*)

the topsoil is a reminder of
that blood

       those reds   (shipping my country out to my country)

            "selling my country out to my country"

⁓

       are you the kind of person who finds scabs beautiful?

           (a scab is a mirror)
           (combined with a time machine)

～

"I believe in art"   ("I buy it")
I bought a train made of pure art &

shipped my steeds
out aboard it,

my all-but-stillborn steer on my art train to slaughter

I paint billboards red
in my sleep

I have never heard of the blues

～

you can't ostracize a man who doesn't care any more
than you can a stone

           (reverberations swirl around your mindless naught)

       here is the pestle rolling around in the mortar hole

       they found out atoms are basically nothing

       & having bullets & bullhead invective & getting shot

           is the same as walking through the universe

           (I can feel planets welling up)
           (they have conscience, same as any loose contrition)

to diverge from the grist requires a double tunnel,
one hole for you, & another

      to dump one's solidarity down

            (I don't question your effort to live; I question effort itself)

      the stone for example has *stone conscience*

argue with that I dare you
that's the mechanism of modern loneliness

                    (ground glass, ground snow)

I am sure I know where this came from   (the man in the mine)
                              (I am pretty, I am sure)

      he is a one-man choir
      omniaudible

                    (much like his money)

~⌒

strippers were there   (of the land)
not tassels, not airline uniforms

airwave forms

                                                    (you think you're so nuanced but what)
                                                    (does that trowel amount to)

   manufacture drools
   over the iron mountain's cleavage;

I touch myself wearing
a thousand pairs of work gloves on my thousand hands

                                                    (we call this "sensitivity")

   you see the alpha male
    humping a grate,

humping a great sword out of a stone
& sledging it back in

                                                    (man is dust, jittering; man is dirt)
                                                    (self-emulating)

~⌒

where are all our parents?   ("out of town")

someone has replaced all the windows with broken windows,

no matter what science says, a stone isn't like an atom

("but men are moles")

all I see is red   (the town has an odor like a guillotine)
                                    (that has just been used)

I see foxes

                        I see no jays
                        I see no music

I know there are starry ratchets wheeling
in the burnt pallet
they are making time   "happen"

~

you are my blue-shifted love, departing;

            I am your blue
            shifted love, stationary,

                                ("who compellingly appears to depart")

the ladle called *creation*
poured me into your mouth,

     pours me there daily   (I am cooling but very hot)

       fission is a state of constant lapse

I know I know, red giantess
as if a man's fist could clench

    so tight it turned to a baby fist

                      (some days I only see pressure; others)
                      (only diminishment)

so my tongue at the center of heaven is a node, & the brain's center
of speech is a living dead muscle

         (a zombie muscle)

      where all the vibrations
      inter-cancel

         (my mouth's an oral harmony so perfect,)
         (so self-complimentary)

         (it cannot be said to exist)

lie here, kiss me, I don't care
what state we are in anymore   (as long as it's a state of grace)

                                                (whose tongue is that, whose bullhorn)

someone's thrown a punch through the stain glass window

                                                (the one that depicts us not acting desperate)

just take one look

at that goddamn handsome mirror

slicking his do back
& making choices

                    (striking out, panning)

                    (panning out, striking)

as the radiator begins to bleed

                                                (bleed sound)

~

Echo is an incision   (my plectrum the incisor)

you can throw music into a lakebed & it won't drown

                        (it can be tied to rocks, even)

~

in the last act I convert

to a million different religions & then convert them into currencies
then convert into pure current

                (like severing yourself from your own face)

                (it takes a lifetime to disown your hometown)

IV.

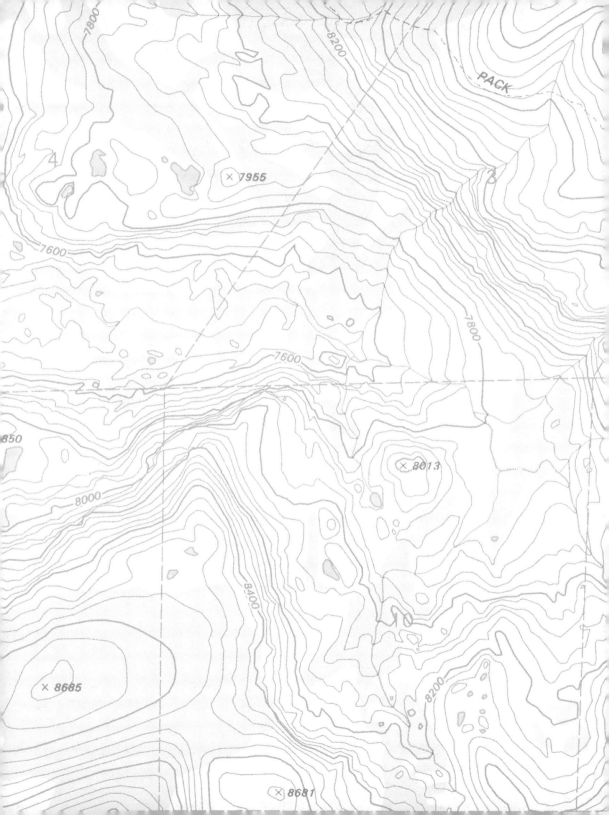

[Narcissus the Paperwhite]

what billows out of the chimney is sunlit, then starlit

(you shouldn't brag)

I think about missing things

but I don't miss them

a hummingbird is a bullet with wings

the flower is a syringe

(paregoric, panacea)

the white pine is ghostly white

with nectar

I must look
perforated,

(like a flower)

I must look like a thousand
   hummingbirds (people in love)

paper

sunlight striates the chimney
you've seen this)

smoke (you think

I must look

like an origami bird
in an origami bud

I must look like the process of folding a flat paper

into a paper vessel

[Terrarium Letter #6]

Sorry I called your book a beautiful shitstorm, it was a compliment, like all the oaks of narrative (that's not a thing) were submerged to the hilts in silt & trod by bombers on stilts : : : You see my book's a very bad state fair itself, born of gawkers & ever unto gawkers, as I say, like all pop music really.

Jesus was an eyesore, any pattern that common (polka dots, polkas, anarchism, anachronism) will fall on its face as soon as the squirt guns lift aloft : : : You should see this paper-cut, fortunately I stabbed the bastard back, you're your own worst editor, har, har.

If I thought the book was a bad shitstorm I would have said as much.

[Notes Upon Completion of a Record]

I could have been any number of horrible things

                            to be boring is a preemptive death
                            worse than death itself

so what

       if I live on a cusp

my eyes' red rims have seen twenty-four hours of day

something beautiful made my ears ring—

ghosts playing steam pipes with immaculate time
I collaborate with dears & dead & resurrected
selves
                (they are smiling)

you are not a family until you play like a family
I want to live forever,

         ears vibrant with phantom bands

I have a good memory & a bad guitar
look at the ember, the reel:

         we are holding hands around a fire where normalcy is burning

[Telegram]

THE CANARIES MIGHT HIT THE WINDOW ONE AT A TIME

LIKE RIFLE-FIRE

OR IN A FLOCK LIKE A SHOTGUN

CLUSTER-FIRE

POINT IS, WE SHOULD START BUILDING WEAKER WINDOWS THAT

BIRDS CAN SHATTER THROUGH

THE DEAD BIRDS DESERVE IT SO DO THE ROWDY BOYS

HURLING LIVE BIRDS THROUGH WINDOWS

WITH NO WINDOWS IN THEM

[Terrarium Letter #7]

Dear Shithead, you know I love you & yes, I'm proud of my failure to fail, I eat two sometimes three meals a day, my height climbs as does my weight as does the jasmine on the jasmine-prone trellis, when you're down I say ignore the atmosphere, you're party to your own magnificence, the only thing between you & the universe is one runt leaf in the blue blue sky (but don't be picky).

To see enough is to see enough, the bud that dreams of being a butterfly is an idiot, the pupa that dreams of being a jasmine are idiots.

But they are audible, they are into sentience, they are on the bough and rocking it, I say rock your failure (to fail) till it "capsizeth."

[*The Dive at the End of the World*]

The board walks into the sea.

You endure the interiority, the breathless cigarette

smoking inside. When I'm not lonely

it's like I was never lonely

(the moon's sun enough) i.e.

I am happy through refraction. The fish

vanish around the curvature of the bottom of the ocean,

soothing the undersides

of boats. A miniature solstice occurs

on either side of sunset;

I fancy I helped its orange strip diminish.

The eye's impressions remain there

close-liddedly,

the canoe bears its horizontal endlessness,

bow & boat curve upward, downward,

sometimes all the pitches

happen in unison: you look to your elbow

& your forearm is attached to it,

sometimes even (*red-light barroom, bar-light,*

the sun's last tongue licking the earth's chops)

your lover is there.

[Notes for a Song Called "The Drift"]

The cottonwoods continue to impregnate one another, meaning
I miss the drift of snow across a prairie,

meaning I miss the drift of kissing you across the plains,
meaning I miss the drift of not ever kissing you at all.

My stargazer friend thinks the stars are far apart
because they wanted to get away from us; I don't blame them

actually of course I do—all we need is a statuesque look
& the patience to breach the breach

between now & the day the radio breaks open
for its tribute to you, to truth, and to yours truly.

[Pastimes]

There are people who identify trucks on the highway by engine sounds,

regional birds by birdsongs. They never catch the trucks, they never catch the birds.
I am skilled in a different useless skill.

The reflection running through my house has my own body,
but I don't find him overly shadowy.

Some days I think I am deaf & just know a lot about hearing.
Some days I could catch him if I want, but I don't want.

[*Terrarium Letter #8*]

"…& then died" is a good way to cut a thematic loss or stop embarrassment from happening, I think I was loving ponies (gray) in the dream, Love isn't always explicit but this time it was, multiform, multicolored

I remember dreams as though they are manes clipped from my neck (I was riding a bareness or baroness), We threw out the wicker chairs because they resembled collapsed houses or, worse, functional houses for collapsed apocryphal straw men

Everyone in dreams is tired of dreams aren't they

My arms get so energetic they desert me, I misbehave like a saddle, that book I read (in dreams) it had crap alliteration

Love me, I commanded "…& then died"

Have you seen your era recently, the news has a face like a bird (symbolic, symbiotic), dirt is more alive than a city but you can't hardly eat either

Madmen construct cinder, blocks, bad manna ("& then died")

Even in death I am multitasking (to paraphrase Whitman), the dream had the word *mimic* in it, like *meme* or *mime*, yes, I'm not illiterate in dreams, I like to collapse into (a poem) a bad chair

In everyone's life the liver is the protagonist ("& then died"), I slept so hard I didn't even know I was alive, you tagged yourself & then I tagged myself

"& then" the book reverses from a book to a stack of pages to a stack of horsemeat (everyone is complicit) to a stack of trees, to a forest, that's how love works

"& then continues working."

Epilogue

[Telegram]

I AM NOT WASTED BUT I WASTED A LOT

OF MY LIFE

ANY PART OF IT NOT RECEIVING ACUPUNCTURE

FROM STARLIT NEEDLES OR

PINEY STARLIGHT

WHEN I LOOK AT MY MUG I SEE NOTHING

MORE THAN A MUG

IT'S A SHAME EVER TO BE NOT SINGING

HELL IT'S A SHAME EVER EVEN

TO SING THE SAME SONG TWICE

LINER NOTES

This book includes a companion album of original music written and performed by the author. To hear the songs associated with *The Stuntman* please visit milkweed.org/the-stuntman

[TRACK LISTING]

1. Never Was a Cowboy *(7:30)*
2. Casey Jones *(6:07)*
3. Seventh Street *(4:01)*
4. Replica America *(5:48)*
5. God's Country *(7:08)*
6. Song to Myself *(6:27)*

[ALBUM CREDITS]

All songs written by Brian Laidlaw
Performed by Brian Laidlaw (*guitar & vocals*), Danny Vitali (*bass & vocals*), J. T. Bates (*drums*), Jake Hanson (*electric & slide guitar*), Alex Ramsey (*piano & organ*), and Brett Bullion (*auxiliary percussion*).
Produced by Brett Bullion
Mastered by Huntley Miller
© 2015 by Brian Laidlaw (ASCAP)

Lyrics, news, and tour dates available at www.brianlaidlaw.com

ACKNOWLEDGEMENTS

"Courtesy Call" & "Notes for a Song Called 'All It Takes'" appeared in *Failbetter*
"The Cartographer Cries into His Knapsack" appeared in *Pleiades*
"If We Dig Up the Overworld" appeared in *Paper Darts Magazine*

To Danny, Lucy & the Doc, for the harmonies & memories
To Ashley, the girl from the North Country
To my professors & cohort at the University of Minnesota MFA program
To Kate Nuernberger, for her brilliant edits
To Daniel Slager, Patrick Thomas & the entirety of the Milkweed crew,
for bringing this project into the world

Brian Laidlaw is a fiscal year 2012 recipient of an Artist Initiative grant from the Minnesota State Arts Board. This activity is made possible in part by a grant from the Minnesota State Arts Board, through an appropriation by the Minnesota State Legislature and by a grant from the National Endowment for the Arts.

CLEAN
WATER
LAND &
LEGACY
AMENDMENT

Originally from San Francisco, BRIAN LAIDLAW is a graduate of the University of Minnesota's MFA program in poetry. His poems have appeared widely in journals such as *New American Writing*, *FIELD*, *VOLT*, and *The Iowa Review*. He has also released several albums, most recently *Amoratorium* from Paper Darts Press. Laidlaw is currently an instructor of songwriting at McNally Smith College of Music. When he is not on the road, he divides his time between the Twin Cities and the Sierra Nevada.

Interior design by Mary Austin Speaker

Typeset in Bulmer

Bulmer is a transitional serif typeface designed by the British type designer and punchcutter William Martin in 1792. Martin studied under John Baskerville, and used Bulmer to set the Boydell Shakespeare folio edition in the 1790s.